A FAN'S GUIDE TO BASEBALL FEVER

THE OFFICIAL MEDICAL REFERENCE

By

Thomas Singer, M.D. and Stuart Copans, M.D.

Designed by William S. Wells

Quote on page 16 taken from *Take Time for Paradise, Americans and Their Games* by A. Bartlett Giamatti. Copyright © 1989 by the Estate of A. Bartlett Giamatti. Reprinted by permission of Summit Books, a division of Simon & Schuster, Inc.

ISBN 1-55935-083-0

Printed in the United States of America

Dr. Singer, a graduate of Princeton University and Yale Medial School, practices psychiatry in San Francisco. He caught the Fever growing up in St. Louis, and — like Stan the Man — bats left-handed in a coiled, crouched stance.

Dr. Copans, a graduate of Harvard University and Stanford Medical School, practices psychiatry in Brattleboro, Vermont. He roots for the Boston Red Sox while reading Franz Kafka.

Mitchell Rose grew up rooting for the Brooklyn Dodgers. When they moved to Los Angeles, he decided to end it all. Instead he became a cartoonist.

DEDICATION:

As a ten year old in 1917, my father, James W. Singer, Jr., read about a triple play in the St. Louis newspaper. He persuaded his father to take him to a ballgame so that he could observe this miraculous play first hand. So began the family infection with Baseball Fever. Although my father has yet to see a triple play after 74 years of watching for one, he still roots for the Cardinals. This book is lovingly dedicated to him, to my brother J. W. S. III, and to my children — Jimmy, Eliza, Sarah and Molly. I also want to mention others with whom I have shared the love of the game: Rus Messing, Yogi Hickey, Dixie Deibel, John Levis, Sandy Galt, Fred Hanser, Denny Wedemeyer, Glen Pritzker, Jason Weinberg, Carolyn Bel, Iden Goodman, Tom Kirsch, George Wilson, Neil Russack, Rick Wright, Gary Fathman, Steve Grand-Jean and Peter Rutter. Finally, a word of gratitude to my beloved wife, Jane, who turned to me in the first inning of a World Series game we had traveled 2,000 miles to see and queried, "Who's playing?"   **Tom Singer**

To my children, especially Roy, who suffers from the Fever. May he live to see the Red Sox win the Series!   **Stu Copans**

This project was looking at a called third strike until Bob Evans, Bill Wells, Mitch Rose, Fran Christie and Pat Hager came along and resuscitated it. We are very grateful.

TABLE OF CONTENTS

CHAPTER 1

Definition

prevalence

Few Americans have escaped the ravages of Baseball Fever. If you've never caught it, then someone very close to you has, and it's as hard to be a relative or friend of a fan as it is to be a fan.

population at risk

Like chicken pox, the Fever is one of the most common diseases of childhood that also occurs in adulthood. Cases have been reported with date of onset as late as the eighth decade of life. Rarely fatal, for many it becomes a lifelong condition.

geographic distribution

In recent years, the geographic distribution of Baseball Fever has spread from both American continents as far afield as Japan and even Russia.

CHAPTER 2

Aetiology

AETIOLOGY

Each spring, something stirs in everyone's bones. If the renewal of the life cycle for you always coincides with the start of spring training, you are a carrier of Baseball Fever. The origin of Baseball Fever has been a mystery puzzling medical scientists for over a hundred years. If Baseball Fever had existed in the Middle Ages, it would have been attributed to divine possession. Whatever the cause of the Fever, most sufferers seek neither relief nor a cure. We discuss below three current theories under investigation.

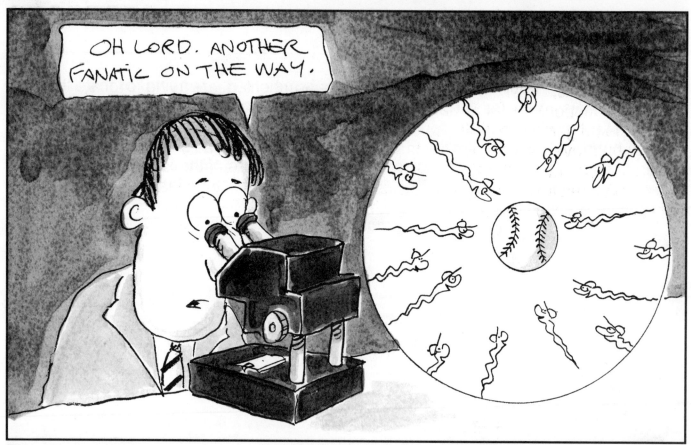

Many scientists, convinced that Baseball Fever is inherited, are trying to locate the specific gene responsible for its transmission. Originally, researchers felt that the Fever was a sex-linked genetic disorder found exclusively in the male population. But this finding has been proven to be culturally biased, and further study has shown that the Fever is equally distributed among males and females. The hope, at least among those who have lost a relative to the game, is that, by identification of the mutant gene, the course of the disease can be halted.

This line of inquiry is known as the "germ theory" of Baseball Fever. Germs include bacteria, viruses, television, and some in-between organisms that can be likened to the designated hitter—not easily classified, but hard to get rid of. There is no doubt that, when Pennant Fever takes hold, something akin to the contagious spread of a disease is happening. The Fever looks, smells, and acts like an epidemic caused by an infectious agent. But, to date, no causative organism has been isolated.

Some psychologists speculate that Baseball Fever originates in the wish for enlarged body parts.

The lack of success among geneticists and infectious disease experts has opened up the field to that illegitimate offspring of modern medicine—psychiatry. Psychological theories range from the belief that the baseball bat represents the penis to the idea that baseball fulfills modern man's search for wholeness—the baseball diamond symbolizing wholeness.

A particularly attractive hypothesis offers baseball as the antidote to the contemporary experience of alienation. Our culture is so obsessed with the moment to moment recording of its every event without discrimination that, paradoxically, you may sometimes lose track of which decade you are wandering through. The team you love gives you a real location in time and space. It provides you with a sense of continuity, an ongoing connection to your homeland and its history.

"So home is the goal — rarely glimpsed, almost never attained — of all the heroes descended from Odysseus.... If baseball is a narrative, an epic of exile and return, a vast communal poem about separation, loss, and the hope for reunion — if baseball is a Romance epic — it is finally told by the audience. It is the Romance Epic of homecoming America sings to herself." A. Bartlett Giamatti

Major league baseball public relations men exploit this longing for connection, especially at World Series time. They are particularly adept at manipulating your feelings if you have moved away from *Home* and become a *Fan in Exile.* And somehow this is everybody because if you haven't moved in space, you still have moved in time. The feelings of a *Fan in Exile* include isolation, uprootedness, and discontinuity. Nostalgic replays of great moments in baseball history painfully tug at these feelings of dislocation and make you long to belong. An advertisement between innings may show a rural farm community gathered around the barber shop radio and, even more impressive, an empty Grand Central Station in New York City—empty because everybody is listening to the World Series. The whole country, urban and rural areas alike, is eternally in the grip of the Fever at World Series time. "Baseball Fever—Catch It!" Big league advertisers know whereof they speak. Through your team, you know who and what you are, and where you come from. You have come *Home.*

CHAPTER 3

Symptoms

DIFFERENTIAL DIAGNOSIS

The symptoms of Baseball Fever are protean. They mimic a number of other illnesses, making a differential diagnosis quite difficult. Like appendicitis, the real threat of Baseball Fever can be masked by vague somatic complaints. Like malaria, its course can be unpredictable and intermittent, with ferocious fever spikes and welcome lulls that ebb and flow over decades. Like manic-depressive illnesses, the mood swings can be intolerable and exhilarating. Like malingering, you can never be sure whether you are dealing with the real or fictitious. To differentiate the many ways in which Baseball Fever presents itself, we have divided this vast symptom complex into five general areas: the physical, addictive, emotional, collective/tribal, and spiritual.

HEADACHES

As every real fan knows, Baseball Fever can knock you out. Once the season gets under way, you may notice an increase in the frequency and intensity of headaches. If you are unfortunate enough to suffer migraine headaches, you may have even observed a phenomenon that we see from time to time in our medical offices. With the onset of spring training, the visual aura that often precedes more "normal" migraine headaches changes. Instead of seeing flashing lights or a double image, you may see thousands of split-finger fast balls winging at you from every direction. This startling spring aura is invariably followed by a crushing headache.

GASTROINTESTINAL DISTURBANCES

Once you settle down in front of the TV or in your seat at the ballpark, you may be besieged by a host of eating disorders and gastrointestinal upsets that literally run the gullet from total loss of appetite to massive overeating. If you eat your way through difficult situations, doubleheaders present dire situations for you, not to mention the people sitting in front of you.

As the season progresses, the symptoms of Fever-induced appetite disorders can intensify. One recent patient checked in with a severe and sudden weight gain. Not until his favorite hitter went on the DL did we uncover the cause. The patient revealed that he had the unshakeable conviction that for every hot dog he ate, his hero hit a home run. Alternately, during a particularly close pennant race, we have seen sudden and massive weight loss in those too uptight to eat. Vomiting, diarrhea and constipation are every day facts of life in the course of Baseball Fever.

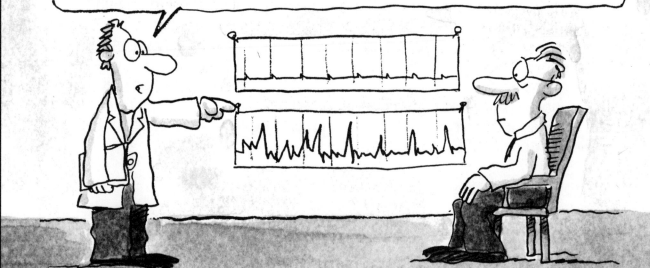

CARDIAC

Tragically, Baseball Fever can break your heart. Cardiac complaints are not infrequent in fans and if your deepest feelings are tied to a team, you are at risk. Cardiac problems present themselves as both real and imagined. Every year a few unlucky fans pay the ultimate price of their passion and suffer fatal heart attacks in the heat of the Fever. On the other hand, you probably have had the experience of your heart missing a beat at a particularly tense moment, only to discover that, as soon as the long drive landed safely in the outfielder's glove, your impending cardiac arrest mysteriously vanished.

INSOMNIA

The onset of Baseball Fever frequently announces itself with a sleep disturbance.

Difficulty falling asleep almost always occurs after a close game in which your team loses by a run in the late innings of a game. It is not only regrets that make it difficult to fall asleep. Anticipatory insomnia is described by many fans who can't stop worrying about the next day's game—overnight trades, pitching rotations, batting orders, upcoming schedules, who's hot and who's not. Victory, however, will generally allow you to sleep like a baby.

Awakening in the middle of the night is sometimes caused by a nightmare. If you can remember the dream, you may find that it involves an improbable but catastrophic plot against your team or favorite player.

FEVER ORGASM

You may be lucky enough to experience a far rarer interruption of your sleep. This symptom attacks both the naive, first-time sufferer of the Fever and the most seasoned pro. Clinically known as Fever Orgasm, this subjectively delightful phenomenon is the baseball equivalent of a wet dream. The content of the dream has an almost universal pattern. Your hometown hero hits a grand slam home run with two out in the bottom of the ninth to climax a 4–3 come-from-behind win. Secretions invariably accompany such an apotheosis and the dream is rarely, if ever, discussed with anyone.

Early morning awakening usually occurs at 4 or 5 A.M., accompanied by a feeling of non-specific dread. An early check of the morning sports section may prevent this uneasy sensation from developing into a full-blown foul mood.

As a rabid fan, you may fondly think of yourself as a bit of a nut but may balk at being put in the same category as a drug addict. During the height of the Fever, your passion may imperceptibly slide into a true addictive process with all the physiological and behavioral hallmarks:

• the need for ever-increasing doses of the desired substance to achieve a short-lived high that is almost intolerably exciting;

• withdrawal of the chosen substance that causes you distressing emotional and physical symptoms which range from restless agitation to panic attacks and delirium.

• recourse to theft to support your habit, ranging from conning kids out of baseball tickets to playing hooky from work and stealing weekends from the family.

To heighten the excitement of the national pastime, you may develop an addictive appetite for betting on games. If it doesn't cost you a place in the Hall of Fame, your scheming may still get you into trouble with your spouse every time you sneak away to place a bet with your bookie.

MEDIA MANIA

The goal of this addiction is to be completely aware of every event affecting your team. As a result, you may become a virtual prisoner of the media—scanning several newspapers a day to get divergent accounts of last night's game, sneaking off to your car to listen to the latest radio bulletins without interruption, ducking into sports bars to check out the national TV sports networks. In the delirious phase of the Fever, you may find yourself calling a sports line talk show to challenge last night's choice of relief pitcher or to express dismay over a rumored trade. The extent of your Fever can be measured by your willingness to endure the talk show host's dogmatic and long-winded response. Withdrawal from the media substance at a critical point in the season when on vacation or business trips can cause temper tantrums, breaking and entering of newspaper racks, or expensive, even transoceanic calls.

CARD COLLECTING

(Including autographs, baseball bats, gloves, and other memorabilia)

This baseball addiction strikes all ages and is often handed down from one generation to the next. The thrill of great profits from valuable cards only adds to the pleasure of possessing the image and statistics of every player in the history of the game. Collecting also has the advantage of keeping the Fever alive during the off-season, when winter trades at the traveling card conventions will feed your insatiable appetite for anything remotely concerned with baseball. Among the addictions available to children, card collecting is relatively benign but awesomely powerful.

ANXIETY

Anxiety is the symptom described most frequently by sufferers of Baseball Fever. You may suffer both acutely and chronically, with panic attacks lasting for one pitch to an entire season. Anxiety can take the form of non-specific discomfort, sweaty palms, clammy skin, nail biting, butterflies in the stomach, facial tics, or the total body variation known as feeling like a bundle of raw nerves.

UNPREDICTABLE VIOLENT MOOD SWINGS

The mood swings associated with Baseball Fever resemble the harrowing roller coaster rides of childhood. Some days you will be filled with inexplicable kindness and joviality to family, friends, and co-workers. You may start the day smiling at total strangers. A few hours later, you are seized by a mean-spirited crabbiness that defies rational explanation. But wait! You suddenly remember that your team blew an important victory three weeks earlier by walking in the winning run. Boisterousness alternating with extreme irritability are sure signs of an elevation in your Fever.

DEFICIENCIES IN CONCENTRATION

You are easily distracted and are unable to concentrate on anything other than a ball-game for more than five minutes at a time.

POWERLESSNESS

You experience inexplicable feelings of hopelessness and powerlessness. You have to discover over and over again that it is not within your power to end the drought of a six-game losing streak despite your deeply held conviction that your listening to, watching, or attending a game can make a big difference between winning and losing. As a diehard fan, you may have as much trouble accepting the fact that your participation has little if nothing to do with the outcome of a game as you have accepting the possibility that your position in the universe is meaningless.

SOCIAL WITHDRAWAL

When your team loses, you become socially withdrawn and refuse to talk to anyone—except perhaps to share your misery with a fellow devotee.

OBSESSIONAL THOUGHTS

Your thoughts become obsessional. You endlessly replay close games in your head. Such circular thinking is usually introduced by the notorious "what if." What if that line shot had been an inch inside the foul line? What if that close call at the plate had been safe rather than out? Your obsessional thinking usually occurs only with a loss. You don't tend to obsess about your victories. Throughout the season (and your lifetime!) you may vividly remember games that should have been won and find yourself constantly recalculating the standings to see where your team would have been if they had won those 22 games they dumped.

COMPULSIVE BEHAVIOR

Behavior can become compulsive as the season progresses. You repeat certain simple, stereotypical actions at specific times throughout the day without the performance of which you are unable to proceed.

MAGICAL RITUALS

Like the cave men who drew pictures of the hunt, you may begin to engage in magical thinking and rituals to guarantee the success of your team. These include wearing special costumes, uttering secret incantations, and even building sacred totems or shrines at which you worship and bring votive offerings. If you are involved in the darker side of baseball magic, you may find yourself casting spells on your rivals with curses that range from the vulgar to the more esoteric. These ingenious activities of the true baseball devotee find their origin in such innocent childhood gestures as crossing your fingers and closing your eyes at a critical moment in a game.

PARANOID THINKING

You may become paranoid and delusional. This is an incapacitating state of mind, usually involving an irrational idea that a hostile force is plotting to do your team in. (Of course, there is always the possibility that your conspiratorial theory is the truth.) You may believe that a TV network is trying to turn the whole nation against your hometown favorites because your team is not located in one of the few TV mega markets. Or a bad call by an umpire that on instant replay is clearly shown to be in error can lead to the fixed and undying conviction that there is a conspiracy to tilt the series to the rival team. Rarely will you have a paranoid delusion that someone has rigged the game on your team's behalf.

EUPHORIA AND ELATION

At times, you may experience euphoria and elation, a heightened sense of excitement and well-being often described as feeling on top of the world. This is a particularly dangerous symptom when the game, the pennant drive, or the World Series isn't over. Of course, if everything goes your way and your team wins it all, you can join hundreds of thousands of new friends in proclaiming, *"THIS IS THE GREATEST DAY OF MY LIFE!*

SUICIDAL THOUGHTS

The omnipotent peaks of invincibility can quickly reverse into a terrible, humiliating defeat. All of your hopes may be dashed in the final moments of the seventh game of the World Series. Your team lets everyone down and, even though there may be pious declarations of gratitude for what it was able to achieve under the circumstances, you may have thoughts of suicide.

HOMICIDAL IMPULSES

If your level of frustration exceeds all normal limits, rather than hang yourself, you may wish to murder any number of people:

- a player on your own team who is a *Bum* for striking out every time there is a runner in scoring position;
- your manager for leaving a tired pitcher in the game just long enough to lose the game;
- a member of the opposing team who is a *Hot Dog* for humiliating your team by hitting a home run and rounding the bases with "one flap down";
- an umpire who changed the outcome of the World Series and all subsequent history by missing the *Big Call;*
- your spouse who doesn't even know the name of the team you're playing against in the World Series and is insensitive to the pain you feel;
- your parents for the world not turning out the way they promised it would;
- your children for switching the channel to Sesame Street and making you miss a crucial play;
- God for allowing evil and suffering to exist.

DESPAIR

After the murderous feelings of betrayal subside, you may be left with a deep inner emptiness and a feeling of profound loss. The world becomes devoid of meaning, like an empty stadium with the lights turned out. Only a long winter hibernation, perhaps a few timely trades, and the renewed hopefulness of spring training may help to heal such deep wounds. Then, like the woman who forgets the pain of childbirth, you may be willing to try again.

INDIFFERENCE

In the wake of a losing season, or just a losing game, you need emotional defenses to protect you against the direct onslaught of anguish. Just as the body releases endorphins to protect itself against the experience of extreme pain, sufferers of Baseball Fever are blessed with a host of reliable inner attitudes that serve the same function—ballorphins. The most common ballorphins follow:

You can give up, and become serenely indifferent—even to the point of not checking the daily scores.

DISILLUSIONMENT

You can become disillusioned with:

• the players for their greed and lack of loyalty. Not only are they in the game just for the money, but their personal lives are a mess and hardly what you want your kids to identify with.

• the owners, who are even greedier and more uncouth than the players. Not only are they in the game just for the money, but they are imperious and self-aggrandizing.

• the owners and the players for their constant haggling over staggering sums of money that mock the salaries and sensibilities of most mortals.

• the game itself. When your team loses you see the reality behind the myth of the *National Pastime*. It's just a big, dirty business peopled with overgrown boys. Through the clear vision of the disillusioned fan suffering terminal Fever, the game itself is revealed as a slow, boring sham fueled by the national appetite for nostalgia, entertainment, and escape.

You can become objective, even philosophical in your thinking, and put the game in perspective through rationality. This thinking takes several forms.

You can dissect the game by studying all the statistics in the history of baseball. This approach can be enhanced by computer-generated graphics and broadcasters filled with endless baseball trivia. When you conclude that your team is outmatched in batting averages, earned run averages, stolen bases, runs batted in, slugging percentages, and has too many ex-White Sox players, you will not be disappointed when it loses.

GLOBAL CONTEXTING

You can think of the game's relative importance in the broader context of the threat of nuclear disaster, ecological catastrophes, earthquakes, and political upheaval in the Middle East. This kind of thinking is a great relief in the face of losing a ballgame, pennant race, or even a World Series.

INTELLECTUALIZATION

If you fancy yourself an intellectual, you may feel especially adept in penetrating the game's mysteries, its subtle rhythms, and its role in mirroring man's fate. Because you are so smart and rational, it is hard to see that you are just as passionately deranged as those screaming "Murder the bum!"

HEARTBREAKER AND STINKER LOSSES

You can handle different kinds of losses in different ways. For example, the heartbreaker can be handled by:

- going to sleep,
- yelling at your spouse or kids,
- getting drunk,
- having sex.

Nothing is worse than the stinker loss, the one that got away through a combination of boneheadedness, ineptitude, and hot-dogging. Nothing helps with the stinker loss, except time. On the other hand, the blowout loss of 21–2 can lead to feelings of relief accompanied by such thoughts as, "We needed to lose one like that and get it out of our system"—like a thunderstorm rolling across the plains, it clears the air.

TRANSCENDENCE

The most serene of all the defenses against recurrent baseball loss is transcendence. Clarity of your thoughts and feelings through meditation allows you to rise above the trials of the less ascended fan.

You are lucky if you suffer from this symptom. It has more grace to it than most. It insures you against almost any setback. No matter what happens, in reality you know that your battered team will somehow resurrect itself—and along the way you—to new and glorious heights of redemption. This symptom is based on a characterological stance that seems impervious to the objective reality of crushing defeat. It is as if the continuing failure of your team only serves to further fuel your eternal hopefulness. Some baseball metaphysicians take this symptom as a manifestation of the desire for the infinite. In their opinion, this desire is the underlying and motivating dynamic of Baseball Fever.

MASOCHISM

Eternal hopefulness can degenerate into masochism. This symptom persists for years, if not for an entire lifetime, and is almost always incurable. Suffering is endless, even when it looks for a moment like you have something to take pleasure in other than your pain. As a masochistic fan, you can always find a way to suffer in victory. You may be lucky enough to root for a team like the Chicago Cubs and share your symptom with an entire city. Sadly, we have been drawn to the clinical conclusion that you secretly love to lose even while overtly proclaiming, "This is the year to win the pennant."

PESSIMISM

Eventually your masochism may give way to pessimism. This symptom is based on the absolute conviction that no matter what happens, even when your team has shone, ultimately it will fail and let everyone down. A familiar refrain issues from your mouth if you are unlucky enough to be stung with this manifestation of the Fever: "I knew they would lose all along." This position is based on the ultimate knowledge of death—the end of the season, the defeat of your team, your own death. The pessimist forgets the rebirth mystery of spring training and takes solace in the reassuring knowledge that everything comes to an end. The credentials of this belief are impeccable. In the end, it is always correct to believe that sooner or later every team loses and every superstar retires—if not this season, next season!

SADISTIC GLOATING

When you give up all hope of your team ever winning, you may console yourself by delighting in the defeat of hated rival teams. Sadistic gloating is particularly delicious if you have an old and close friend who is a fan of that team. In the name of giving your friend a hard time, you can playfully torture him by "rubbing it in." Your enjoyment of his suffering may temporarily relieve and reverse the pain and humiliation you have endured. This friendly teasing can get totally out of control. When you return to your senses, you will be mortified to discover that your behavior was not unlike that of a child who tortures animals for fun.

SPOILING AND EXPLOITING

As a victim of Baseball Fever, you are an excellent target for those who enjoy spoiling your pleasure and exploiting your pain. These misanthropes love to see the home team lose, feign indifference to glorious triumphs, and are quick to capitalize on your vulnerability by teasing you or suckering you into bad bets.

NOSTALGIA

The bittersweet longing of baseball melancholia is one of the Fever's most dreadful symptoms. It reaches back into your prehistory with an aching fondness that reeks of loss. It can present itself as a diffuse mood shrouding you in a mist of undefined mournful feelings and poorly shaped memories. Or it can get quite specific with detailed images of childhood friends and games, sandlot heroes and goats, the long-since demolished stadium that housed mythological confrontations between ancestral giants of the past, now old, fat, or dead. With the Fever comes memories of the house and street where you grew up and the glorious victories and ignoble defeats of childhood play. What do you yearn for when the nostalgic phase of the Fever sets in? A simpler, less harried world that you imagine was the past? The safety of a more innocent age when a ballgame was time standing still on a hot summer day, as endless and eternal as youth itself, until one day you wake up and can hardly remember it?

THE TRIBAL SPIRIT

Your baseball team bears the tribal spirit of the community. The team becomes your personal totem, your family's totem, and your town's totem—a source of hope, inspiration, pride, reverence, awe, or scorn and disregard, depending on whether the spirit (and the standings!) are moving in the right direction or not. You identify with the totem, usually symbolized in animal form on banners, caps, and uniforms. You worship the totem and by its spirit are bound together in a most intimate manner to other members of your tribe.

PSEUDO FEVER

When your team is hot, the Fever becomes contagious. You are joined by thousands of others who suddenly come down with an acute case. This, of course, raises that most despised variant of the Fever: pseudo-fever. Every real fan knows how to diagnose the pretenders who jump on the bandwagon with all the pretensions to legitimate loyalty and devotion. Their Fever lasts as long as the team looks good. You can sniff them out in no time at all and they deserve all the scorn you can muster.

CONTAGIOUS SPREAD

When the Fever strikes your city late in the summer, it knows no bounds. The individual and community spirit is subject to the Fever's unpredictable and gyrating course. To chart the trends of such a collective seizure is far more difficult than keeping batting averages and E.R.A.s. Keeping track of an individual's Fever chart is relatively simple compared to the wild fluctuations of a city seized by the Fever. What does it take to set such a phenomenon in motion, to infect an entire region with an unidentifiable agent that turns everyday life upside down and strikes with such protean symptomatic manifestations? Your team must be a contender!

ANTI-FEVER

It is rare for the Fever to spread through the community in the face of mediocre play or ongoing defeat. Nevertheless, the Fever can become rampant even in the face of catastrophic loss. This happened in the 1988 season when Baltimore lost its first 21 games! A wonderful, rarely seen form of the Fever broke out locally and then nationally—a kind of anti-Fever with all the hallmarks of a real Fever, except that the precipitating agent was the sweet smell of loss rather than of victory. Under more normal infectious circumstances, however, the Fever only takes hold collectively when your community sees a chance to participate in a pennant race.

PROCLAMATION

As it becomes clear that your team has a chance for a division title, newspapers, radio, and TV literally begin to proclaim the Fever in their headline stories. This signals the onset of an epidemic.

STRANGERS BONDING

Once the Fever takes hold of the community, total strangers begin to exchange kind greetings on the sidewalk and conversations unfold on elevators, replacing averted eyes with active mouths. This drives diehard, cynical fans crazy. They sneer in the face of such "Have a nice day" inanities, and would even prefer to lose than jump on the Fever-induced bandwagon of self-indulgent congratulations.

MYTH MAKING

A collective myth of your team begins to take shape in the consciousness of the home-town fans and the nation. The myth usually includes all the elements of a mystical jour-ney. Heroic figures face enormous adversity on route to the ultimate confrontation with the dragon. On the way, there are internal and external demons, hardship, injury, and at some critical moment certain death. Miraculously, unexpected help comes from inferior journeymen, cast-off players who rise to the occasion and prevail in the face of over-whelming odds (including those of the bookies). The highlights of the season become the fabric of a great tale to be added to and embellished by hype and years of retelling.

FEVERISH BEHAVIOR

Your behavior at games (and at home in front of the radio or TV) takes on feverish qualities as you join cause with thousands of people waving little white hankies or huge towels—all with a tremendous sense of fun, purpose, and destiny.

FATE OF THE REGION

Your city begins to feel that its entire history and fate is on the line. Economists tell everybody how much money is pouring into the city, but as a real fan suffering the Fever you pay little heed to that. You know the Fever transcends mere economics. Money belongs to Caesar; the ballgame belongs to the gods. The upper midwest, for instance, always seemed destined to lose the big one in both football and baseball until the Minnesota Twins reversed the fate of the region in 1987.

SHADOW PROJECTION

When gripped by the Fever, crowds take on sinister as well as joyous qualities. This is caused by a particularly virulent symptom of the collective/tribal aspect of the Fever, the projection of the enemy or shadow onto the rival. The opposing team's region begins to take on all the qualities that the native region despises and disowns. In the 1987 National League playoffs, St. Louis became a "cow town" to the San Francisco fans, while the Cardinal fans spread the malicious rumor that the Giants' slugger Jeff Leonard secretly "ate quiche." Feelings ran much deeper than the stupid sloganeering would suggest. Indeed, in this phase, the Fever can become quite nasty. Temperatures of whole regions run at dangerously high levels, threatening to turn sport into war and sportsmanship into hatred as has happened with European Soccer Fever (ESF).

UGLINESS OF CROWDS

Local media jocks, including carping sportswriters masquerading as columnists, are particularly good at fanning hatred. The ugliness spreads to crowds seized by the Fever. In this symptom cluster, taunting, ridiculing, harassing, even physical violence break out. Mocking slogans, gloating fans, and vicious personal attacks become the norm in a Fever-crazed crowd.

MONSTERFICATION

If you get caught up in this phase of the Fever, you can become something of a monster yourself, although you are likely to believe it's the other team's fans that are behaving like jerks. One sportswriter described such fans as looking like the Turkish extras used in filming the prison scenes of the movie *Midnight Express.* In this agitated frenzy, you can lose sight of the grace and compassion that normally accompany your sense of sportsmanship. Anything becomes an acceptable way to achieve victory. Indeed, victory becomes sweeter if the arch rival is injured, degraded, and humiliated—not unlike ancient Mayan hoop games in which the loser is sacrificially slain at the conclusion of the game. With the cosmos itself split into good and evil, your very existence and the tribe's very existence hangs in the balance of the mother of all battles to defeat the awful (or wimpy) enemy.

PEAKING TOO EARLY

This is a very common and enormously upsetting tribal symptom, usually experienced by you in the most personal and shaming way in the midst of a screaming crowd. It begins with a rising expectation of victory that is uncontainable. A kind of collective premature ejaculation takes place as the crowd gloats in the fantasy of a quick and easy kill. The visiting team's slugger faces a 3-2 count with the bases loaded and the home team already comfortably in the lead. As the slugger falls to his knees swinging wildly at the third strike, a maddening roar carries you, as part of the feverish crowd, to unimaginable heights of ecstatic pleasure in the climax of victory.

COLLAPSE

In the very next inning, your pitcher walks a man with two outs and nobody on and subtly shifts the momentum of the game. Before you know it, the floodgates of hell have opened. In the seeming blink of an eye, the game has been tied and now your team is trailing by a run. Everybody is stunned. As if a switch had been thrown somewhere in the ozone, the crowd goes instantaneously silent and limp as it watches the glorious triumph slip away. Only if you are the most seasoned, controlled, and perhaps soured, fan can you escape the excesses of peaking too early by guarding against premature arousal.

CROSS REGIONAL FEVER BOND

As the tribal warfare of a pennant race or the World Series peaks, you may experience a phenomenon opposite to the perception of the opposing team as the enemy. We have given this strange reaction the clinical name Cross Regional Fever Bond or CRFB. The immunology in this rarely reported symptom is a total mystery. It occurs when a fan of the rival team recognizes you as a fellow sufferer or vice versa. Spontaneous support groups emerge, although you would never call them that. To date, no formal Baseball Fever Anonymous organizations have sprung up. With CRFB, the sense of your shared fate as a victim of the Fever is stronger than regional rivalries. Your affliction unites you in deep mutual understanding and respect with some unlikely soul mates. This symptom can be most disturbing because you are forced to recognize that a fan of the team you hate the most is also a human being. For that reason CRFB is a very short-lived, transient phenomenon.

SPIRITUAL SYMPTOMS

There is a spectrum of symptomatic manifestations of Baseball Fever. At one end of the spectrum are physical symptoms, and at the other, spiritual symptoms. Schematically, you can imagine a continuum of expressions running as follows:

PHYSICAL ↔ *ADDICTIVE* ↔ *EMOTIONAL* ↔ *TRIBAL* ↔ *SPIRITUAL*

All of these symptomatic manifestations can shade into one another, and they can have an individual or group expression. For example, increasing urination as an expression of the Fever becomes collectivized between innings, at which time great hordes of people can be seen to disappear beneath the stands. All sorts of information, opinions, and feelings get exchanged, especially in the later innings of the game. The feverish possession is heightened and becomes more tribal in the sharing. At times the Fever crosses over from the tribal into the spiritual dimension and awesome events occur that are rarely experienced in more formal places of worship.

498 FT.

MASS HALLUCINATIONS

This symptom is similar to the mass hallucination which occurred a few thousand years ago when the chief shrine of the ancient cult of Aesclepius (from which modern medicine derives its symbol of staff and snake) was moved from Greece to Rome. Thousands of people witnessed in awe as a 100-foot high snake—the chief god of the cult—slithered out of the temple it was abandoning and made its way down to the boat that was transporting it to Rome. Many Dodger fans had such a vision when Walter O'Malley led his team out of Brooklyn and headed west to the land of the sinking sun known as Chavez Ravine. Sufferers of Baseball Fever have seen more of these events than can be documented: Willie May's great catch, Stan Musial's five home runs in an afternoon's doubleheader, Kirk Gibson's miraculous World Series home run. If you worship at the temple of baseball, you have witnessed things that no one else could understand or believe.

SACRED TIME

Your experience of time shifts dramatically in the acute phase of Baseball Fever. In this heightened state, a kind of delirious excitation takes hold in which every moment of every game grabs you as if it is the first and only time in the history of man that such an event has happened. In the language of theology, the ballgame becomes a *once-and-for-all event*. You have the experience of participating in the moment of creation. Participation in sacred time is one of the great gifts of the Fever, even if to the outsider it may look like Boring Time.

LIFE AND DEATH EVENT

At this intensified spiritual peak of the Fever, what happens to your team becomes a *life and death event;* the outcome of the contest determines the fate of the individual and the tribe. Late in the season, if you are still a contender, every game becomes a cosmic struggle in which all the forces of the universe are brought to bear. The importance of these games for the true fan is matched only by the suffering of Christ or the temptations of Buddha. The most insignificant event, such as a mundane telephone call, may become monumentally decisive in this holy drama and tip the balance.

DELICATE BALANCE

For example, one of our patients made a transcontinental call to his brother as their team entered the ninth inning of the seventh game of the World Series with a comfortable lead. Victory seemed in hand and our patient was confident. The brother receiving the call, equally feverish in his fantasies of deliverance, was outraged that such a pivotal moment in the universe's evolution could be interrupted in such a carelessly dangerous way. He snapped a prophetic warning into the receiver and hung up abruptly: "If they lose the series now, it's your fault." The brother making the call cowered through the final inning, knowing that if their team blew the game, the fatal reversal would have been caused by his sacrilegious insensitivity to the delicate balance of conflicting cosmic forces. Fortunately, this did not become a second Cain and Abel story. The team held on and no blood was spilled.

DIVINE INTERVENTION

In the mystic quest for ascendence over all other teams and union with the holy World Championship, anything that tips the balance against your team is attributed to every extraordinary force other than the opposing team's skill. Feverish fans are quick to spot bicoastal, if not global, television network conspiracies. God and many of his lesser agents join Fate, the Furies, Demons, and the Umpires in jinxing short stops, making a terrible call, delaying crucial games with cloudbursts, and all too rarely letting your team win the *Big One.*

TAOIST FLOW

This sublime state of being—all too rare and even sweeter for that reason—puts you in touch with the natural rhythm of life. On a soft summer day when everything is exactly where it belongs, Baseball Fever allows you to become one with the relaxed crowd, the green grass (or even the astroturf), the warm sun, the blue sky, and the handsome players. All weave together in a seamlessly integrated dance of perfect balance. The harmonious feeling that accompanies this easy flow of man in tune with nature can only be described as serene. Baseball Taoists will tell you that a single experience of it lasts a lifetime.

"axis munditis"

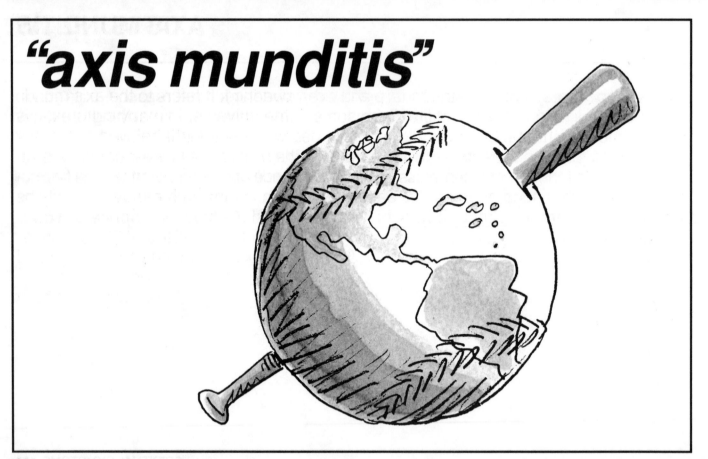

AXIS MUNDITIS

This is a spiritual symptom of the most profound importance. It refers to the axis mundi, which symbolizes the central and unifying force in the universe. In many cultures, it is represented by the world tree or central axis that unites the earth below and the sky above. It holds everything together. Symptomatically, Baseball Fever can cause an inflammation at this center of your being; the basic health and integrity of your organism is either secured and renewed, or devastated. Sufferers of the Fever know that what is happening in baseball is at the center of the universe. Middle East and South American crises, airplane crashes, the stock market—they do not exist or are of minor consequence. In the midst of the Fever the idea that other people including your spouse and neighbors don't even know much less care what is going on in baseball is inconceivable. It hurts very deeply to discover that your own central concern hardly registers in another's thoughts.

TRANSFORMATION

In the long term, your spouse's indifference to today's game becomes of little importance. If you suffer deeply and truly enough, personal and communal transformation is possible, and life is renewed. Transformation is different at different times of life. As a child, the Fever gives birth to the image of yourself as a hero or heroine, able to go forth into the world and slay the dragon, if not the Mets. In your middle years, you can recapture youth, initiate your own children into the spirit of the game, and find new meaning in community participation. And if the Fever burns long enough and is suffered deeply enough, a very salutary outcome is a transformed spirit—*a wise old fan of baseball*—a truly philosophical soul. This rare bird has been around long enough to embrace all phases of the game, including the bitterest rivals. He and she just love the game and through it, life.